CHAMPS!
INSPIRATIONAL ANIMALS

Hero Horses

CHERRY LAKE PRESS
Ann Arbor, Michigan

by Joyce Markovics

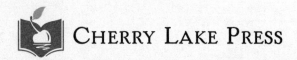

CHERRY LAKE PRESS

Published in the United States of America by Cherry Lake Publishing
Ann Arbor, Michigan
www.cherrylakepublishing.com

Reading Adviser: Beth Walker Gambro, MS, Ed., Reading Consultant, Yorkville, IL
Content Adviser: William Tavolacci, LVT, CCRP Team Leader, Integrative and Rehabilitative Medicine Department, Schwarzman Animal Medical Center

Book Designer: Ed Morgan
Book Developer: Bowerbird Books

Photo Credits: © Volodymyr Burdiak/Shutterstock, cover and title page; © PJ Photography/ Shutterstock, 5; Photos provided by Auburn University College of Veterinary Medicine, 6 and 7; © TristanBM/Shutterstock, 9; © OlesyaNickolaeva/Shutterstock, 11; © Walkin' Pets, 13; © Abbphotography.com, 15 and 17; © Jozef Klopacka/Shutterstock, 19; © Zuzule/Shutterstock, 21.

Cherry Lake Press is an imprint of Cherry Lake Publishing Group.

Library of Congress Cataloging-in-Publication Data has been filed and is available at catalog.loc.gov.

Printed in the United States of America

Note from publisher: Websites change regularly, and their future contents are outside of our control. Supervise children when conducting any recommended online searches for extended learning opportunities.

Contents

Pogo the Pony

Pogo the pony may be small. But he has a big will to live. The little horse was found stumbling along a road in Alabama. Rescuer Shelley Jones knew he needed help. "The pony was in really poor **condition**," Shelley said. "Pogo had lost his left rear hoof." Shelley later learned that dogs had attacked Pogo, causing the damage. And yet the little horse had survived. "I have never seen a horse fight so hard for its life," Shelley said.

Pogo's injury made it hard for him to walk. Shelley thinks he was living on his own for about 6 months.

A horse's hoof is a large single toe with a hard covering. It's made from the same stuff as a person's nails!

Shelley got in touch with a special team of vets. At first, they didn't know if they could help Pogo. But "Pogo was a strong and **determined** fighter," said Shelley. The vets **operated** on the leg. Then, after it healed, they fit Pogo with a **prosthetic**.

It was hard for the pony to get used to his new **limb**. But, over time, he **flourished**. Pogo is a "super pony," Shelley said. She has plans for Pogo to help children who have **disabilities**. "He will not be a pet. He has a much larger mission than that," said Shelley.

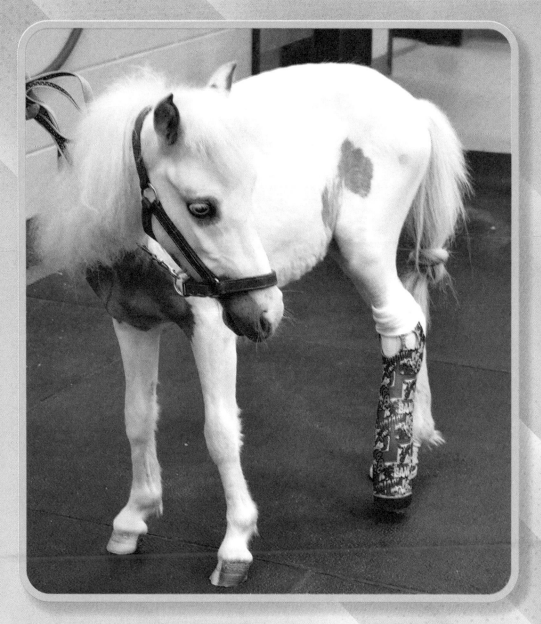

Pogo using his new prosthetic leg

Therapy animals help people who have disabilities and other issues.

Extra Special Horses

Pogo had a leg injury that caused his disability. Other horses are born with disabilities. Having a disability can make it hard to do certain things. Some of these things include walking, seeing, hearing, and learning.

In the past, disabled horses were often **euthanized**. Today, things are different. There are many ways to assist these special horses. With the right support, horses with disabilities can live happy, healthy lives. And they can make great **companions**.

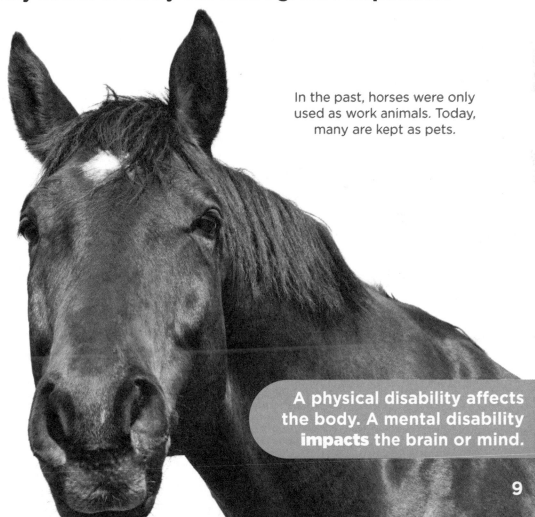

In the past, horses were only used as work animals. Today, many are kept as pets.

A physical disability affects the body. A mental disability **impacts** the brain or mind.

Super STRONG

Teaspoon is one mighty mini. When this miniature horse was 5 months old, a snake bit her. The snakebite caused the **tissue** in her leg to die. To save her life, the leg was **amputated**. A company called Walkin' Pets saw Teaspoon's story online. They build **mobility aids** for pets. And they wanted to help the tiny horse.

Ponies include different breeds of small horses. Miniature horses are even smaller than ponies.

This is a very young miniature horse. Young horses are called foals.

Walkin' Pets helped build a special cart for Teaspoon. It was the first of its kind ever built for a horse! The cart supported Teaspoon's body while her leg healed. Once she was strapped in, the mini took her first step.

Teaspoon's rescuers were blown away. After one step, she took another and then another. The tiny horse quickly **adapted** to her new wheels. Every step of the way, Teaspoon has shown that she's a fighter!

Teaspoon uses her wheelchair for the first time!

Walkin' Pets makes different kinds of wheelchairs and carts. Each one is specially made for an animal and its needs.

Like Teaspoon, Endo the Blind is a fighter. He's also a world record holder! When Endo was young, he had a painful eye disease that caused blindness. To end his pain, vets removed his eyes. "Right after surgery, Endo was scared," said Morgan Wagner, his owner. She found him shaking in his stall. So Morgan stayed and comforted him. After that, she led Endo around the barn until he felt calm. With Morgan at his side, Endo soon got his **confidence** back.

Endo the Blind and Morgan have a very trusting relationship.

Touch is one of a horse's most powerful senses. Horses also have a strong sense of smell and good hearing.

More than 10 years later, "Endo is able to do anything a sighted horse can do," said Morgan. He **competes**, goes on trail rides, and even jumps. In fact, he won a Guinness World Record for jumping. His highest jump was almost 4 feet (0.3 meters)!

Endo the Blind beat other records too. Morgan couldn't be prouder. "Endo has a big personality, that's why I picked him," she said. Morgan is glad to show the world that blind horses are "still capable of anything."

Endo the incredible blind horse

Endo has a best friend named Cinnamon, a mini horse!

To the Rescue!

When a workhorse named Pat lost his sight, he almost lost his life. The farmers who owned him planned to send him to a **slaughterhouse**. Thankfully, a rescue group bought Pat. The group, Pan Equus Animal Sanctuary (PEAS), cares for farm animals in need. PEAS gave Pat a loving home. They also provide homes for 45 other horses! PEAS is one of many rescue groups that help disabled horses.

Horses and people can develop strong bonds.

Equine Advocates is another rescue organization. They care for more than 75 horses. Many of them have special needs.

Henry's Home rescues horses—and people. They welcome **veterans** and first responders to their sanctuary. When he found Henry's, veteran Carlos Santoya struggled with his mental health. "I was a mess," he said. But spending time with the horses gave him hope. "I was able to unwind and let go," said Carlos. At Henry's, both the horses and people can heal. "Our horses are so special," said one of the sanctuary's workers. "They love us, and we love them right back. It's a relationship that you can't match."

Horses need lots of space to exercise.

First responders are the first people to arrive at emergencies. They include firefighters and police officers.

Adopting a DISABLED Animal

Animals with disabilities aren't often adopted. Here are some reasons to welcome a disabled animal into your home!

- **Save Lives**
Because of their special needs, disabled animals are more likely to be euthanized in shelters. Pet adoption can save lives.

- **Companionship**
Disabled animals provide companionship. They can form very close bonds with their human caregivers.

- **Special Abilities**
Animals with disabilities can have hidden strengths. For example, a blind animal may have enhanced senses of hearing and smell.

- **Inspire Others**
Adopting a disabled animal might inspire someone else to do the same!

Glossary

adapted (uh-DAP-tid) changed in order to face new settings and challenges

amputated (AM-pyoo-tay-tid) cut off from the body because of an injury or infection

breeds (BREEDZ) types of certain animals

companions (kuhm-PAN-yuhnz) good friends

competes (kuhm-PEETS) tries to get or win something

condition (kuhn-DISH-uhn) general health or physical fitness; shape

determined (dih-TUR-mind) had a strong will to do something

disabilities (diss-uh-BIL-uh-teez) conditions that make it hard to do certain things, such as walking, seeing, or hearing

euthanized (YOO-thuh-nyezd) painlessly ended the life of a suffering animal

flourished (FLUR-ishd) did well

impacts (IM-pakts) strongly effects something

limb (LIM) an arm or leg

mobility aids (mo-BIH-luh-tee AYDZ) tools that help an animal or person move

operated (OP-uh-reyt-uhd) performed a medical procedure on, often by cutting into the body

prosthetic (pross-THET-ik) an artificial device that replaces a missing body part

slaughterhouse (SLAW-ter-house) a place where animals are killed for food

tissue (TISH-yoo) a group of cells that work together to perform a function

veterans (VET-ur-uhnz) people who have served in the armed forces

Find Out More

BOOKS

125 Animals That Changed the World. Washington, DC: National Geographic Kids, 2019.

Eschbach, Andrea, and Markus Eschbach. *How to Speak Horse*. North Pomfret, VT: Trafalgar Square Books, 2012.

Jazynka, Kitson. Gallop! *100 Fun Facts About Horses*. Washington, DC: National Geographic, 2018.

WEBSITES
Explore these online sources with an adult:

Britannica Kids: Horse

Endotheblind.com

National Geographic: Horse

Index

About the Author

Joyce Markovics is passionate about books and animals. She would like to thank Morgan Wagner and Walkin' Pets for helping disabled animals live fuller, happier lives. Joyce dedicates this book to her mother, a phenomenal equestrian, who died April 1, 2023.